Guitar
beginners
and improvers
music book
revised edition

Tunes
from basics
to baroque and blues

Some other books by Al Summers

Creative Music Manual
(Luniver Press, 2009)

So you want to be a full-time guitar tutor?
(Luniver Press, 2006)

From *Theory Lessons in a Booklet* series:

Modebusters' Handbook

Theory of Music Dictionary

Chord Construction and Interval Busters' Handbook

Chords That Matter

Know Your Notes

and, with Ray Bradfield:

On The Slide - slide guitar handbook
(Luniver Press 2006)

Al Summers & Ray Bradfield

Guitar beginners and improvers music book
revised edition

**Tunes
from basics
to baroque and blues**

**Luniver Press
2012**

Published by
Luniver Press
Beckington, Frome BA11 6TT

www.luniver.com

Digital version
www.gandamusic.co.uk

British Library Cataloguing in Publication Data
A catalog record is available from the British Library.

Library of Congress Cataloguing in Publication Data
A catalog record is available from the Library of Congress.

Al Summers and Ray Bradfield.
Guitar beginners and improvers music book (Luniver Press 2012)

ISBN-10: 1-905986-38-6

ISBN-13: 978-1-905986-38-5

Ray's foreword

We've put together this collection of beginner's guitar pieces as a result of Al's many years' experience of using them and our subsequent collaboration on successful evening classes for adult beginners.
It's designed to be easy to read and pieces are presented in clear settings of both TAB and clef notations.
And they work - as we have demonstrated many times!
Both formats have their advantages and disadvantages: for a beginner without any musical knowledge, TAB is a way of getting you playing immediately; it's 'music by numbers'. It works well if you know the song or tune already, but isn't ideal for showing the rhythm detail of an unknown piece.
Clef notation can better show you this. There are several publications which will show you how it works.

There's no substitute for using this book with a good teacher though, as a teacher can explain techniques and concepts which will make your learning easier and quicker.

Enjoy them. They do get progressively more advanced, so by the end of the book you'll be playing tunes which will sound quite impressive and enable you to join in with other players. Take the chance to do so; playing with others really speeds up your progress and develops another very important musical skill: listening. Listen to *what* you play and *how* you play it; a simple tune played really well is far more satisfying than a more complicated one played badly!

Ray Bradfield 2011

A note about the 2012 revised edition

We have made minor amendments in the text, some small improvements in the layout of a few pieces, and added a new bonus piece at the end. Otherwise, the book remains the same, in its proven format.
We are delighted at the positive, grateful and encouraging feedback that we have received from students and teachers about the book, confirming its effectiveness.
For instructional audio-visual support, visit www.alnray.co.uk

Al & Ray 2012

Al's foreword

This collection began as a series of workshop classes
for beginners in the early 1990s.

The workshops became very successful and grew, the
material being influenced by participants: popular pieces
were retained, others added.

There were soon three sets of 10-week classes.
Collating these as progressive booklets for the learners,
the material continued to change in response to feedback
from learners as well as the other tutors, schools and
music shops who started to use the course.

Beginners don't always know what genre they will enjoy
best and like to explore many types of tune. Melody is the
main focus, chords being physically more tricky for many
starting players. Common guitar notations are presented
from day one, as are enharmonics, and different ways of
showing some techniques. Music has always been printed
in a variety of ways: getting used to how it can look is part
of learning...so this book is inconsistent and celebrates that!

There are some fairly corny tunes here at times.
It is useful to play tunes we know extremely well.
This gives us a chance to listen to our own playing,
evaluate it - and enjoy it.
Much music tends to use the same basic notes so every tune
we learn will help us learn others in very different styles.
Try to resist any temptation to skip pages: everything is here
for a good purpose, to help you become a better player!

This is a repertoire book for those starting out playing.
It does not teach you to play: there is no substitute for
a good tutor, even if you go your own way once you have
mastered the basics. It is a book of tried and tested
material that people of all ages respond to and tell us
they like and that many teachers confirm really works.

Al Summers 2011

contents

a brief list of what goes
on inside, for reference

introduction/dedication

To learn to play an instrument well we need good posture.
We also need to learn good practice: effective approaches
to playing as musicians and as technicians of our chosen
instrument.

This is what good teaching will help you do.

Familiarity is a key to becoming a fluent player: spend plenty
of time and focus playing the guitar. No one else can spend
this time for you.

This book can help.
It presents a large amount of material selected and arranged
to help you gradually attain fluency.

There are many instruction books: this isn't one of them.
You can use this collection with such a book - and/or, better
still, a tutor - to supplement your learning, giving you many
tunes to encourage good musicianship and secure technique.

Chord 'window' diagrams are pictures. The lines represent
strings and frets, the dots show where fingertips go.

TAB is a picture, quite an old one, having been showing
musicians what to do with their fingers for centuries.
It was good for lute players and is good for some aspects
of guitar playing still. The lines represent strings (the one
at the bottom being the bottom, lowest sounding, thickest
looking string), the numbers tell us where our fingers go,
a zero representing an open, or unfretted, string.

Clef notation is a code. The dots of the five-line 'fence'
(stave) tell us what the notes are: we learn their names
and how to transfer that to our particular instrument.
No need for fear: learn gradually, just as we learn what
road signs tell us.

This book is dedicated, of course, to the hundreds of
people who have already enjoyed learning from using
this material - and to all those who do so in the future.

finger exercise

Do this as a warm up every time you pick up the guitar!
Try it on every string.

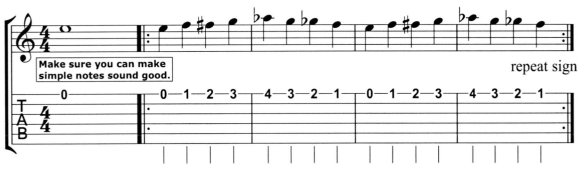

picking pattern

1 Good for string skipping and exploring the *sound* of the notes of your instrument.

chord pattern

You can play lots of songs with these - mainly 4-string - chords.

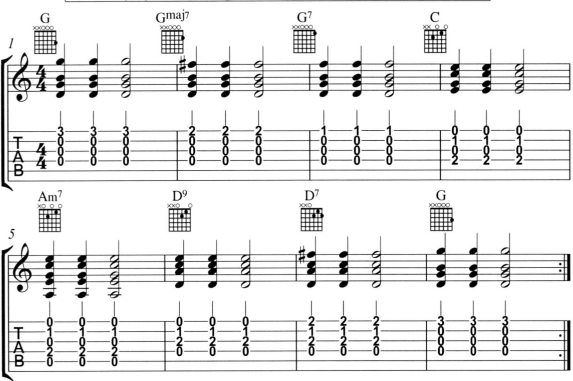

clock chime

To begin, try tunes that you know really well. Really listen to your playing.

It's surprising where this can crop up:
Blink 182 have used a similar phrase!

the number of low Cs tell what hour it is...

There's a fly in my ice-cream

Listen while you play: you may know this by another name.

The beamed pairs of notes are called quavers, or eighth notes.
A beam between notes halves their value, doubling the speed.

London's burning

This piece is in triple time: the three means there are three beats in each bar. Like the last tune, this begins with two quicker notes before the first main bar.

A partial bar at the start like this - often just one, two or three notes - is called an *anacrusis* or 'pickup'.

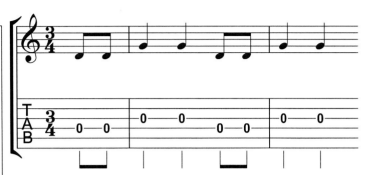

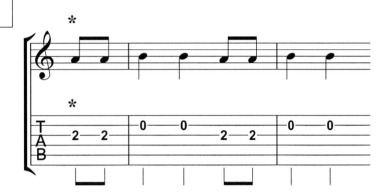

The little squiggle sign is called a rest and tells you to make a silence for one beat.

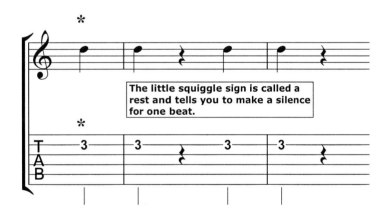

This can be played as a round and is laid out here to show how.
Each * is the point where the next guitar joins in from the beginning.
Each line of music shows a whole phrase.

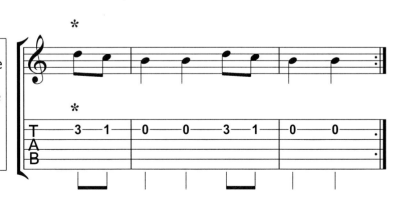

What shall we do with...
...the drunken sailor?

Rhythm: if you can say it, you can play it...

"Bear ti-ger bear ti-ger bear bear bear bear"

...here, "bear" represents a one-beat note, "tiger" two half-beat notes and "sloth" - sounding like 'slow' - represents the longer, two-beat note.

"bear bear bear bear slo...th slo...th"

See also page 44

The Irish washerwoman, part one

The 6 is divided into two 3s. Stress [accent] the first note of each beamed group of three, to make a jig-like rhythm.

Am

Hold the A minor chord shape with the fretting hand, making it easier *and* a smoother sound.

Am..

try repeating it...faster...

Old Joe [based on *Old Joe Clarke*]

14

The lower sounding [thicker] strings are usually called the bass strings.
Bass parts often, but not always, move slower than melodies.
The four strings of a bass guitar have the same letter names as the four
bass strings on a 6-string guitar - E, A, D, G. On a bass guitar they are
even lower sounding versions of these notes.

bass part for *Old Joe*

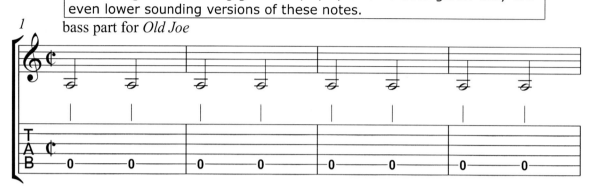

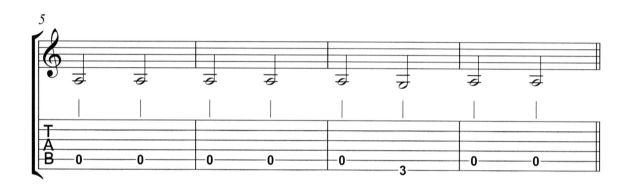

chorus

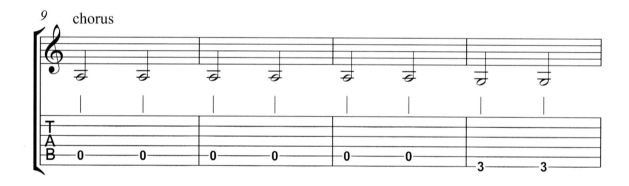

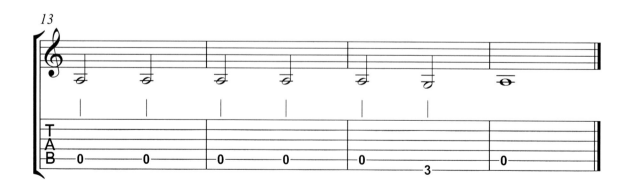

The banks of the Ohio

See also page 51

There are some new chords here. Try to use logical fingering and refer to a chord book if necessary.

traditional

Ah! Vous dirai-je, maman

This has many names and is a tune that has stood the test of time, being also the basis for *What a Wonderful World*.

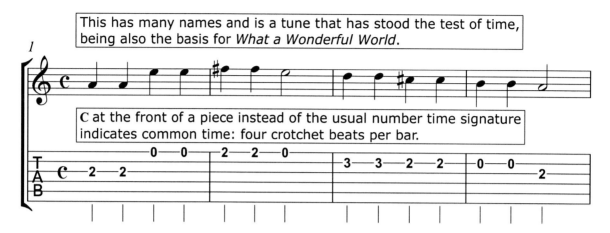

C at the front of a piece instead of the usual number time signature indicates common time: four crotchet beats per bar.

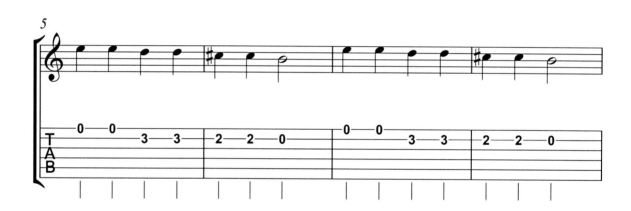

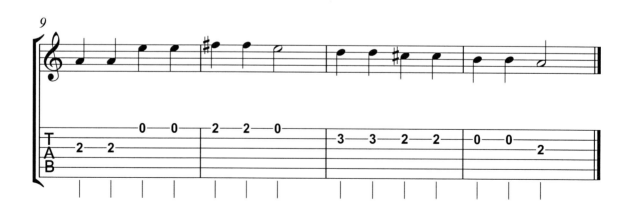

Oh when the saints

Many of the phrases here begin with a
crotchet - single beat - rest, which means
the first beat of the bar, the 'one', is silent.

"Andante"

means - "at a walking pace"

See also page 50

a melody by
Ferdinando Carulli

18

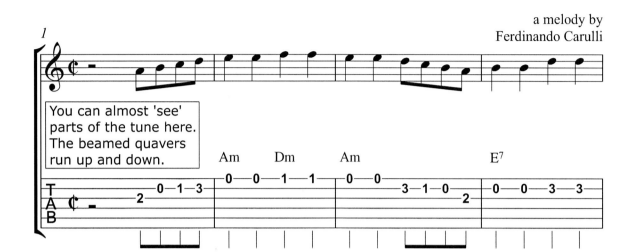

You can almost 'see' parts of the tune here. The beamed quavers run up and down.

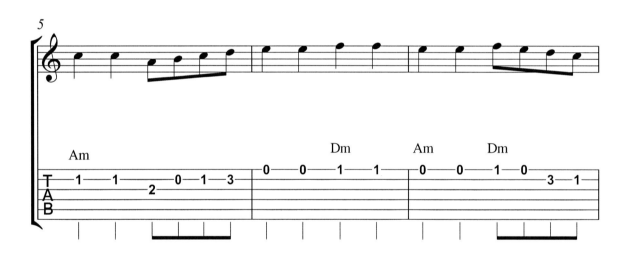

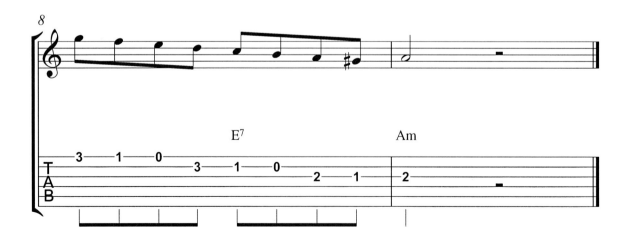

3 Blind Mice Blues - shuffle rhythm*

*Say 'Humpty' or 'Dumpty' to get the beamed quaver rhythm.

a duo part for *3 Blind Mice Blues*

20

a roots bass part for *3 Blind Mice Blues*

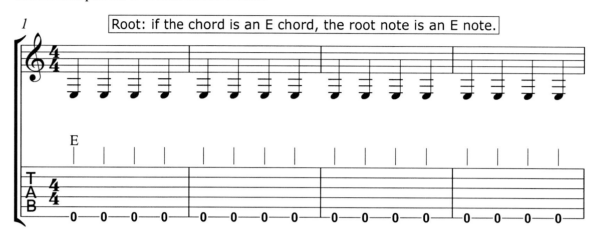

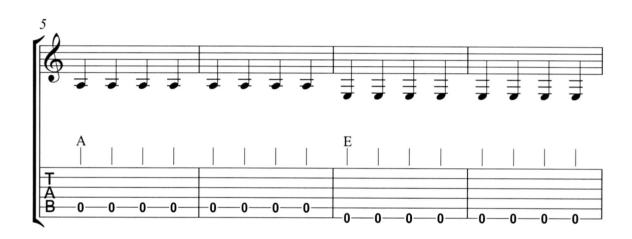

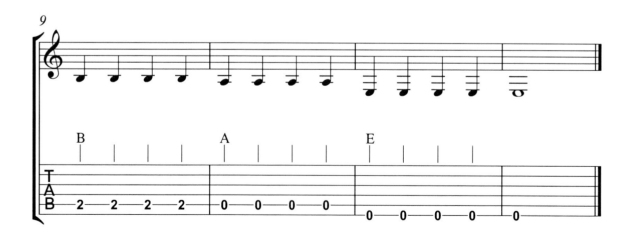

a boogie bass part for *3 Blind Mice Blues*

See also page 43

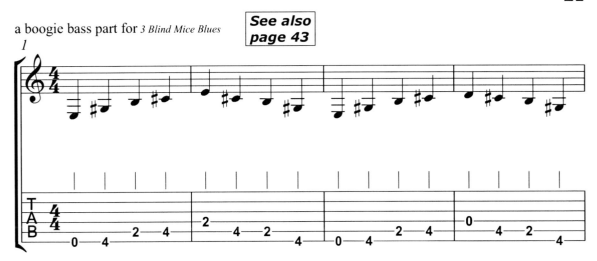

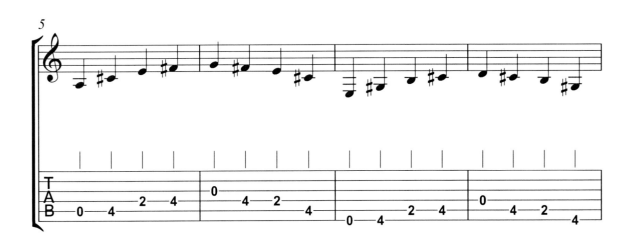

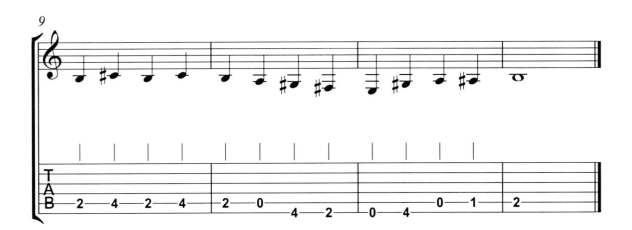

Menuet theme

based on J P Krieger,
a chord sequence used since by composers
of jazz standards, Santana, Gary Moore etc

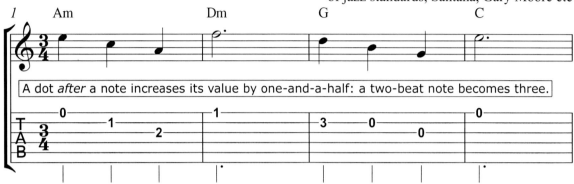

> A dot *after* a note increases its value by one-and-a-half: a two-beat note becomes three.

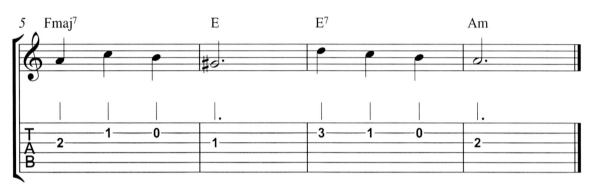

bass for the *Menuet* - with a suggested slightly jazzy chord sequence

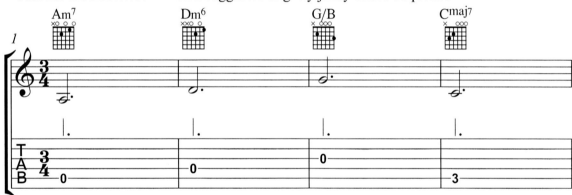

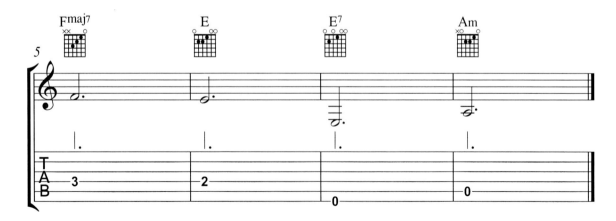

picking exercise in G
in quavers [eighth notes]

See also
page 9

see page 9 for a strumming chord sequence to match this

It's about time to know your notes! - all the plain notes on the first 4 frets:
- a sharp sign (♯) adds a semitone (fret) to the frets indicated;
a flat sign (♭) subtracts a semitone.
So the final G here would be fret 4 if sharpened, fret 2 if flattened.

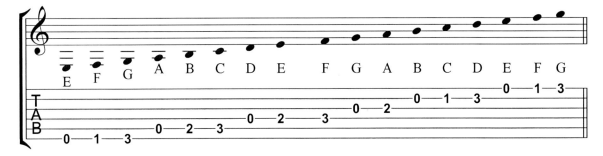

12-bar in A: 5ths with 6ths 'bounce'
see also page 35

Quite bluesy. Try a shuffle rhythm too with this - see page 19.

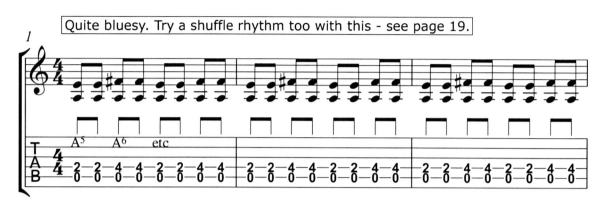

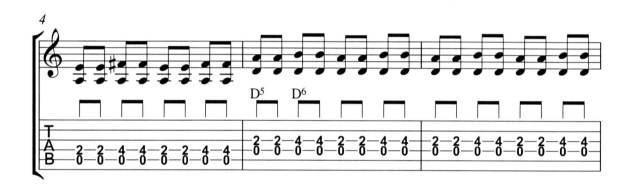

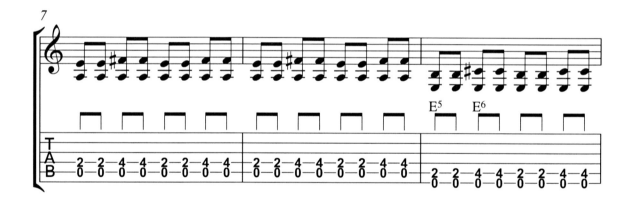

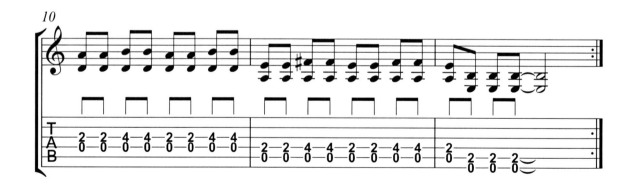

some open position scales:
explore some improvising [make up some tunes and riffs] with these;
do you have a favourite?

minor pentatonic scales in A

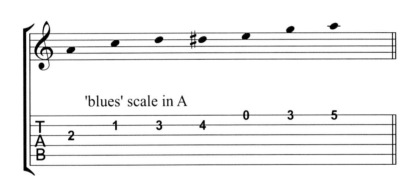

'blues' scale in A

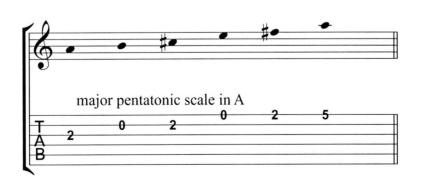

major pentatonic scale in A

Greensleeves
melody

See also
page 54

Seth's tune

Seth Cox

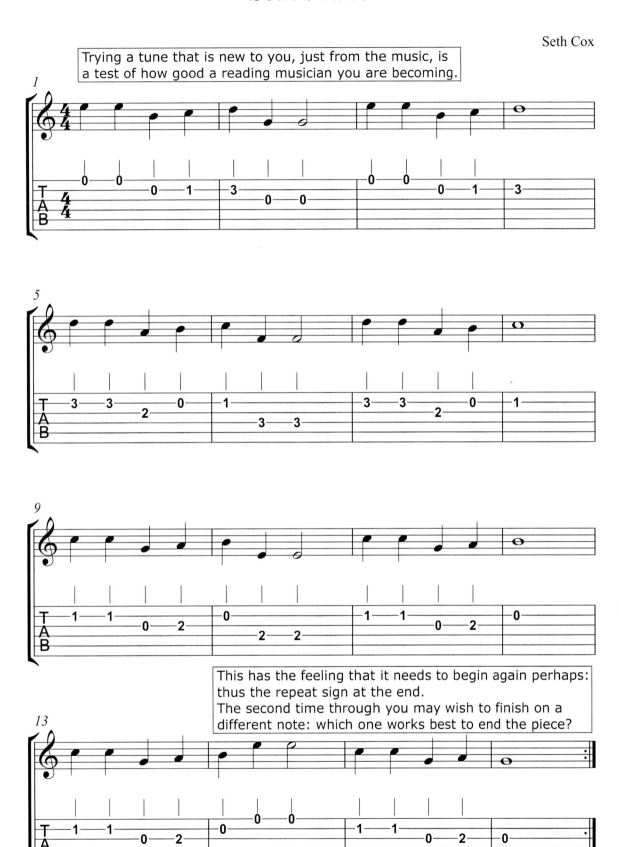

Trying a tune that is new to you, just from the music, is
a test of how good a reading musician you are becoming.

This has the feeling that it needs to begin again perhaps:
thus the repeat sign at the end.
The second time through you may wish to finish on a
different note: which one works best to end the piece?

Turkey in the straw

...and the same tune embellished with notes as 'fillers'; later there are some slurs, shown by the curved lines. The fretting hand articulates the note, by hammering on or pulling off, for a smooth sound.

Boogie in G

high version

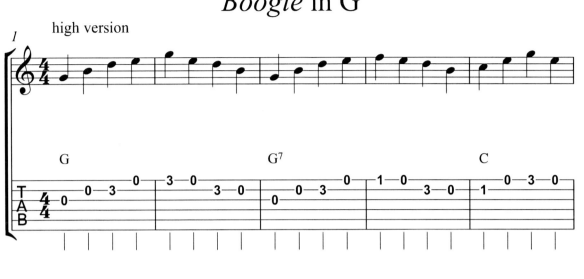

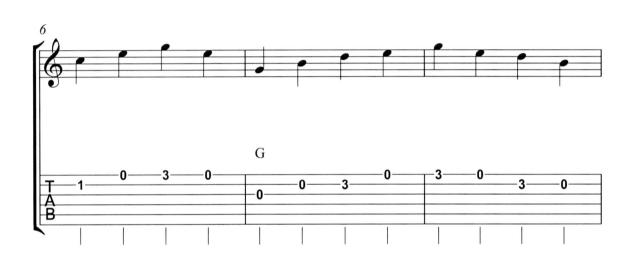

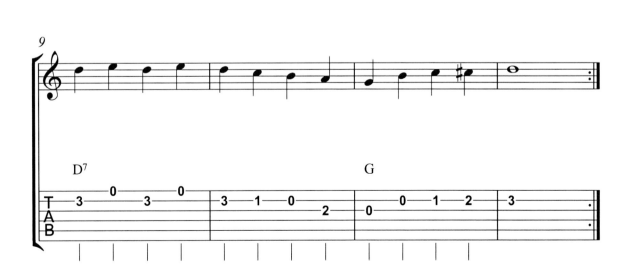

Boogie in G

a low version: not quite the same all the way through as page 29 - they work well as a duet...

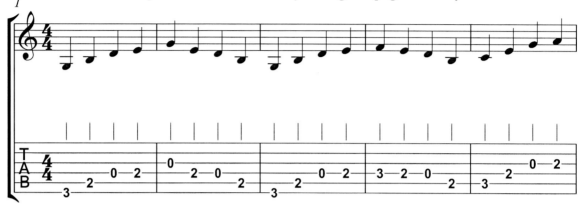

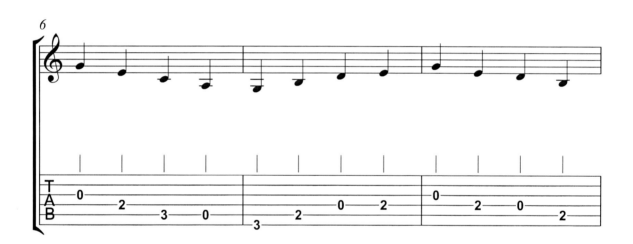

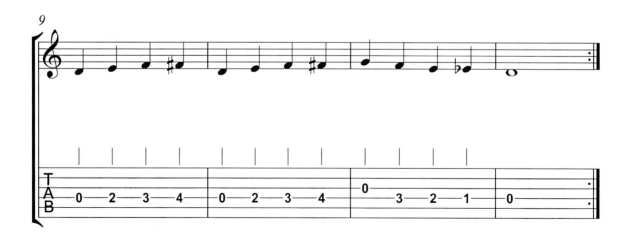

dyads [two-note chord voicings] for *Boogie* in G

Valsette

Al Summers
homage to Bartolome Calatayud

See also pages 58, 64

Harmonic - a sweet and delicate sound made by just touching the string without pressing, just over the fret itself.

harmonic

Valsette - accompaniment

Elise's tune - a Beethoven *Bagatelle* melody - arrangement for guitar

See page 32.

low string *Boogie* in C

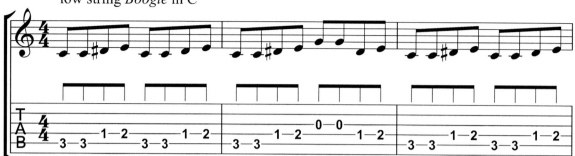

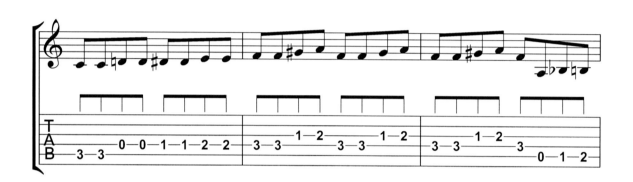

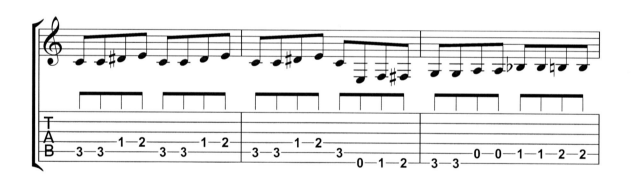

12 bar in A with 5ths, 6ths, 7ths
see also page 24

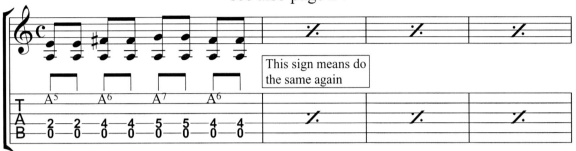

This sign means do the same again

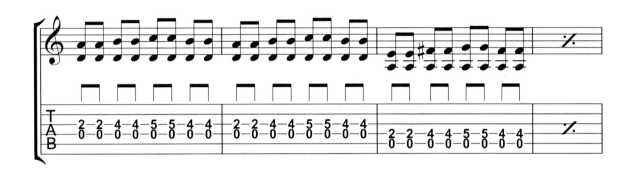

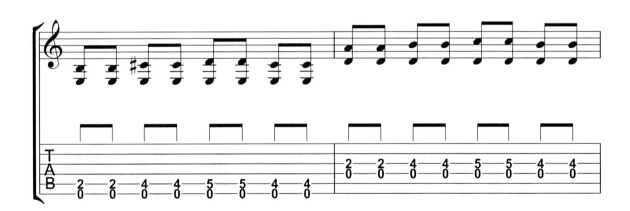

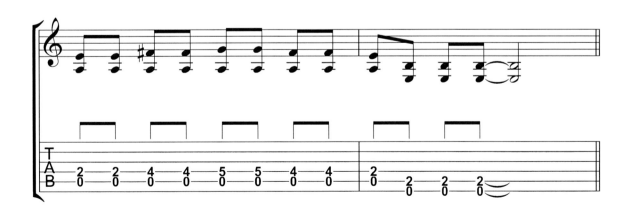

12 bar in E, with some scale ideas on page 37

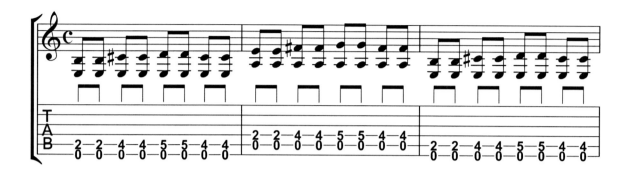

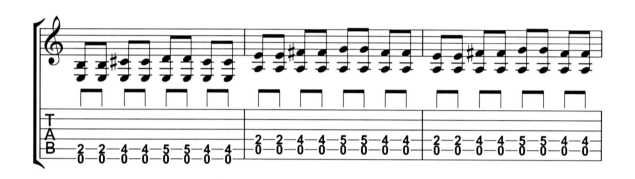

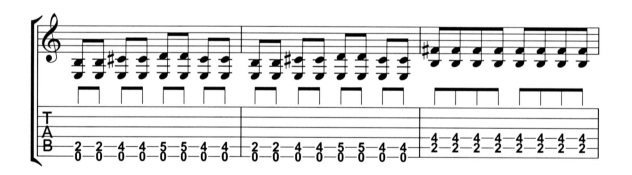

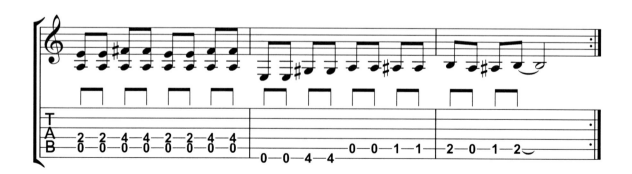

E minor pentatonic scales

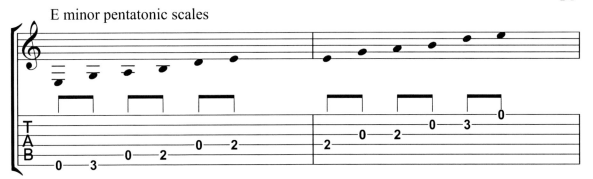

E 'blues' scale

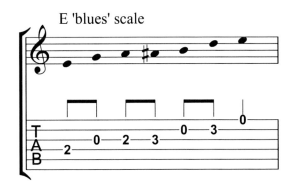

E major pentatonic

gliss is short for *glissando* - slide the finger from one fret to the next, keeping pressure on the string, making a continuous smooth sound...
...often shown as just a straight line between notes

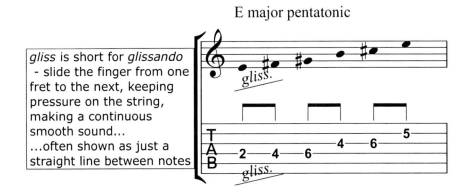

E m pent. [higher position]

E maj pent. [higher position]

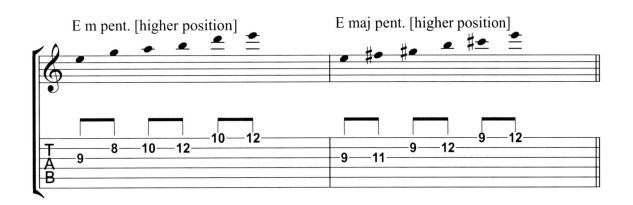

12 bar blues in G - try the shuffle rhythm "Humpty Dumpty..."
for fingerpicking style

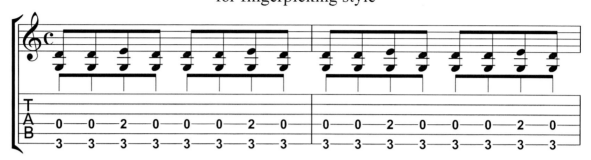

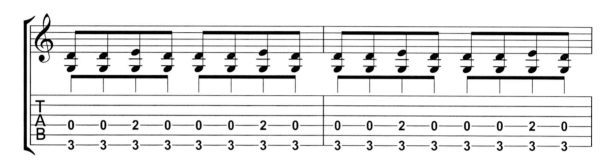

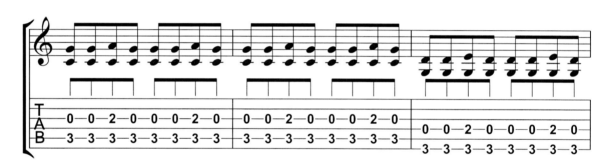

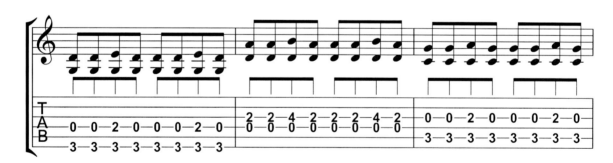

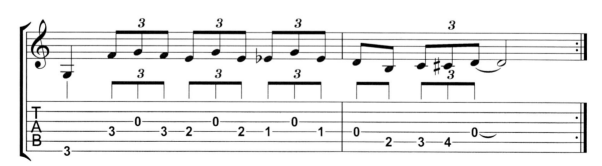

a jitterbug swing - an evolution
how to build a riff, bit by bit
- any version, from about 4. onwards, works

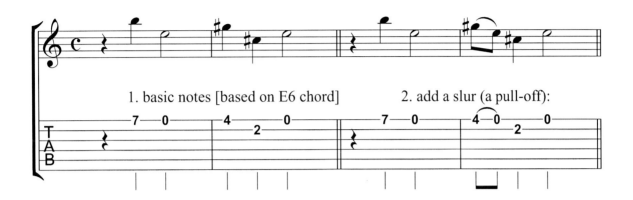

1. basic notes [based on E6 chord]   2. add a slur (a pull-off):

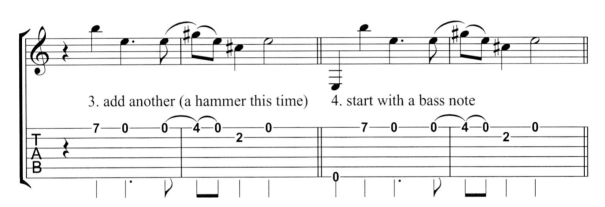

3. add another (a hammer this time)   4. start with a bass note

5. add a bass note at the end to help the flow

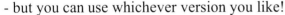

6. finally add a bass note in the middle to help keep it moving & sounding more complete
- but you can use whichever version you like!

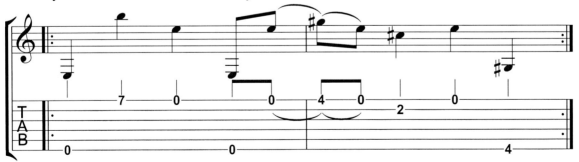

Au claire de la lune

with filler notes

- spot the tune, as it's a little hidden in places here...
...and try accenting the main melody notes

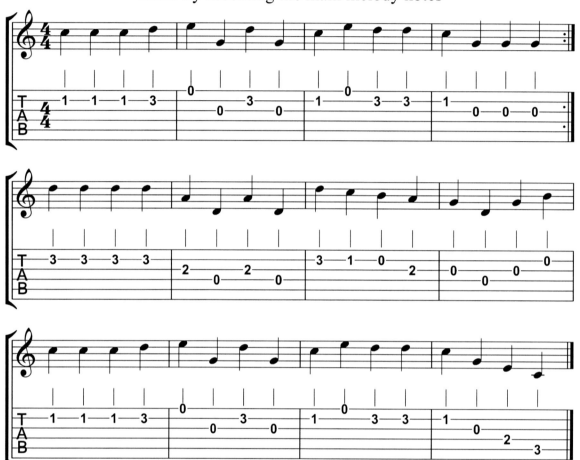

Tash's waiting room music

Natasha James

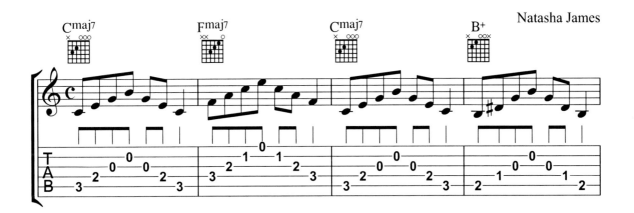

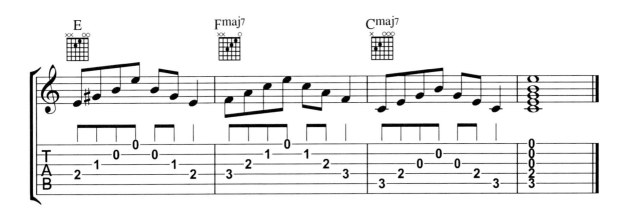

**See also
page 79**

BG workout

Charlie Head

try picking the introduction with the thumb to get it working...

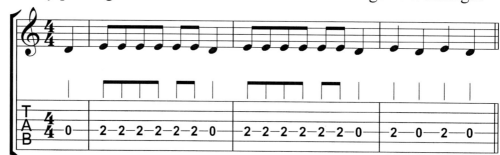

The italic letters here indicate picking hand fingers:
p - thumb [Spanish = pulgar]; *i* - index finger; *m* - middle finger.

p i m i   m i m i

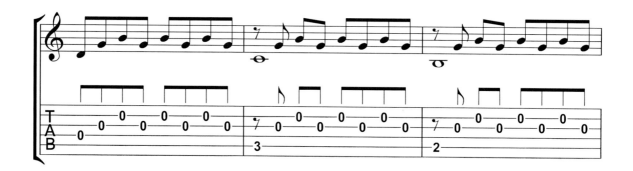

Em

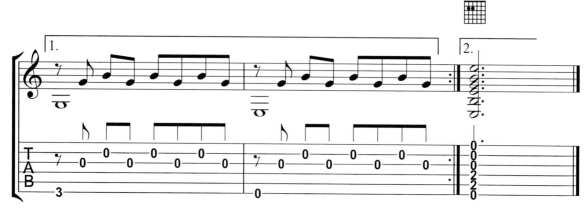

See also
page 21

simply spicing up your boogie:

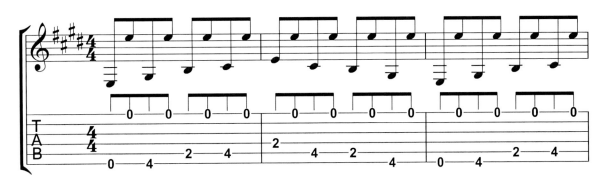

There is a key signature here: the four sharp signs at the start of each line.
This tells us to raise all Fs, Cs, Gs and Ds by a semitone [1 fret].
The natural signs during the piece change some of these back.

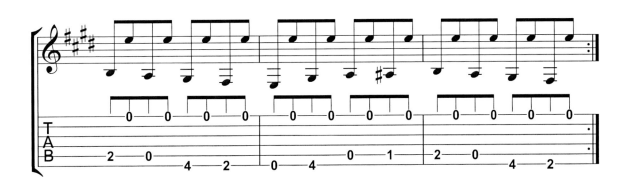

The Irish washerwoman (full version) See also page 12

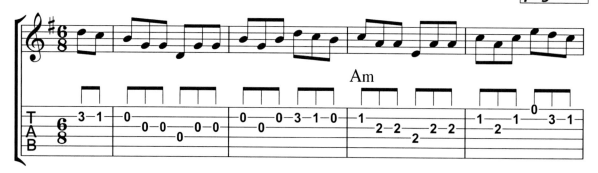

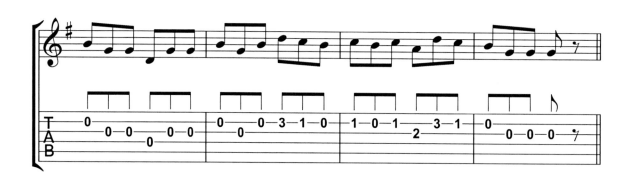

part 2

try repeating it...faster...

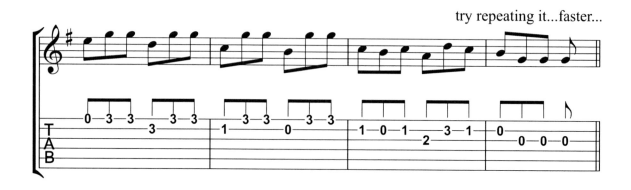

Jake, the scribe, his tune

Only two beats in each bar here.
The quavers make it seem busier!

some variations on a team piece
written at Oaksey village's
Shake, Make and Create project,

Scarboro' fair in D minor

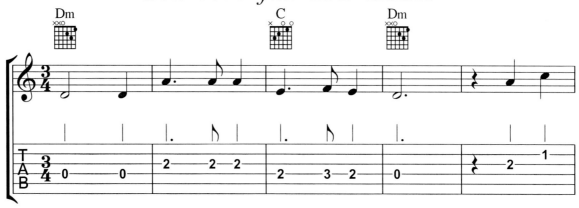

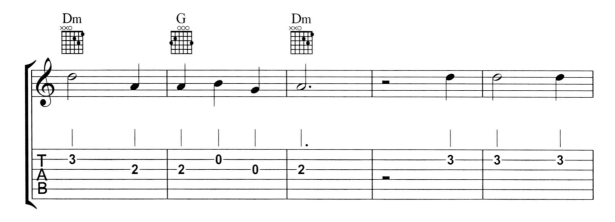

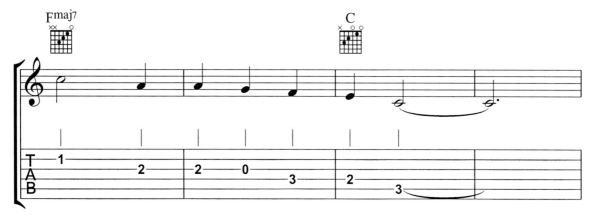

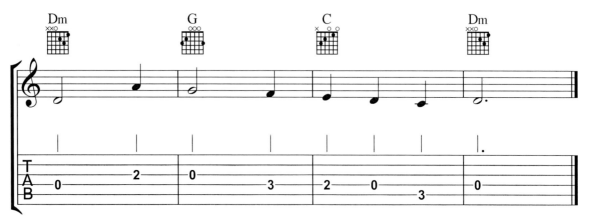

picking pattern for page 46

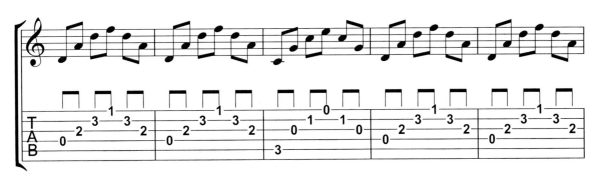

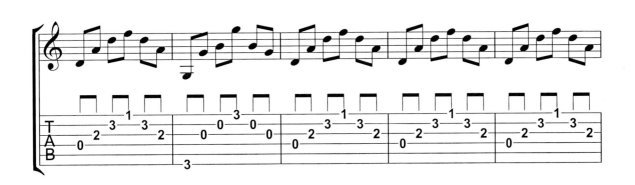

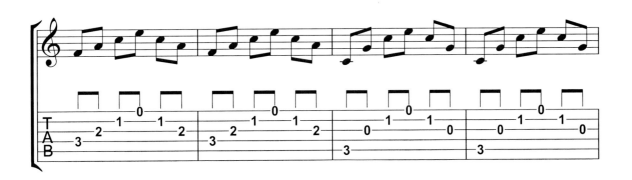

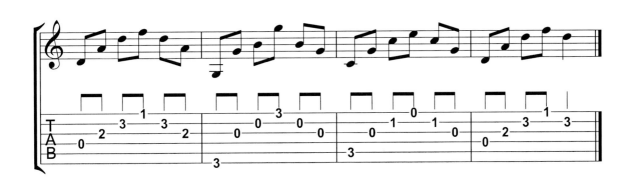

Scarborough Fair in A minor

picking pattern for page 48

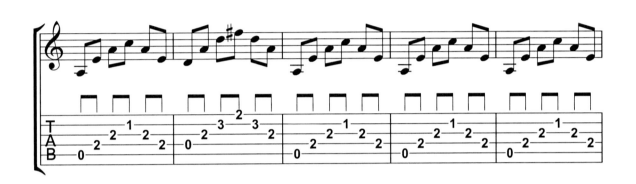

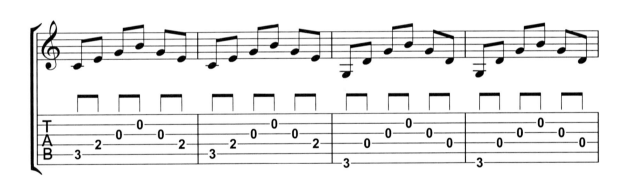

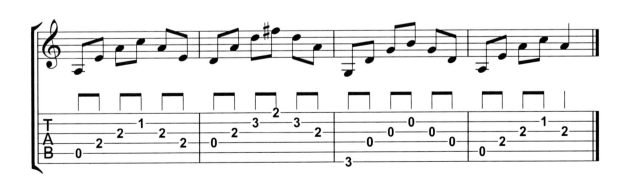

50 *Andante* revisited. This uses the same tune as on page 18: practise the main chords first...

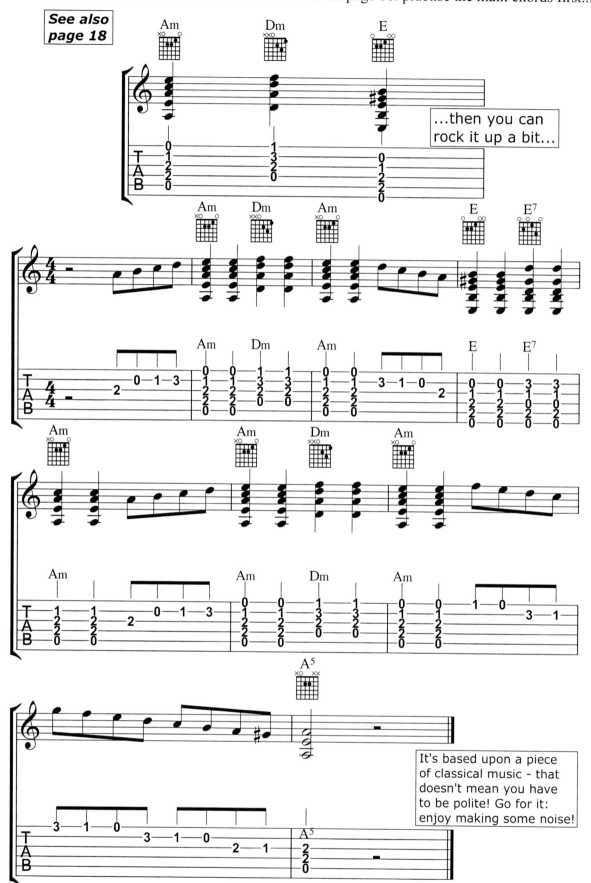

...then you can rock it up a bit...

It's based upon a piece of classical music - that doesn't mean you have to be polite! Go for it: enjoy making some noise!

The banks of the Ohio, with self-accompanying chords

See also page 15

Try strumming each chord just once to give you time to change, then add more strums.

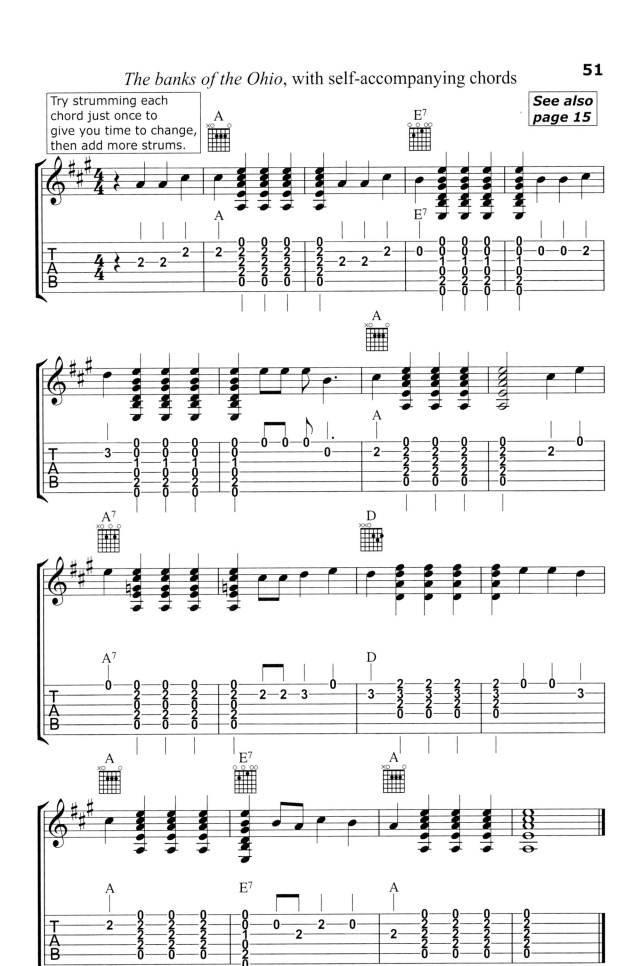

Whiskey in the Jar

an arrangement of a traditional tune
with 'wandering thumb': move on once you have mastered the first bar...

practise this first bar
of thumb picking first

You will almost certainly know this one
...brother who?

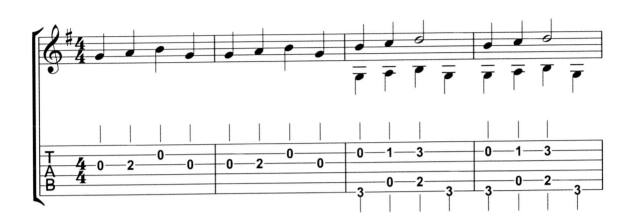

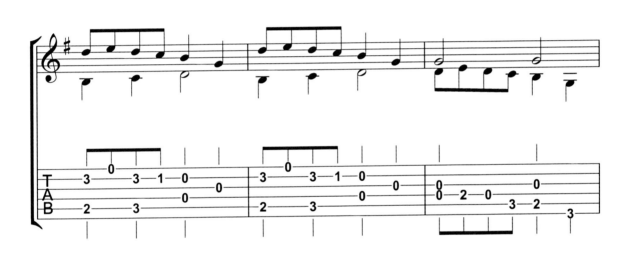

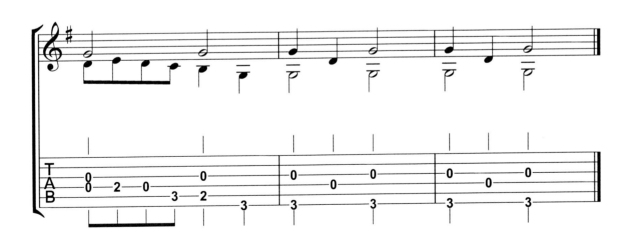

54

See also
page 26

Greensleeves - an arrangement, with bass note suggestions

Just for fun:
a couple of little extracts from Pachelbel's *Canon*

Begin slowly.

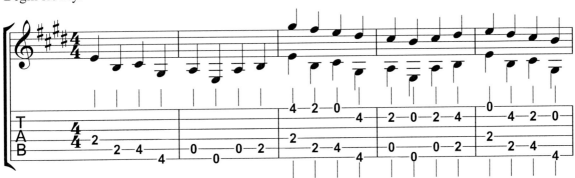

Every time a beam is added it doubles the speed!

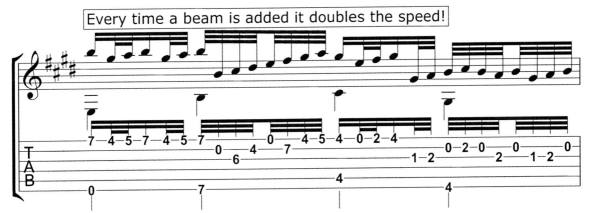

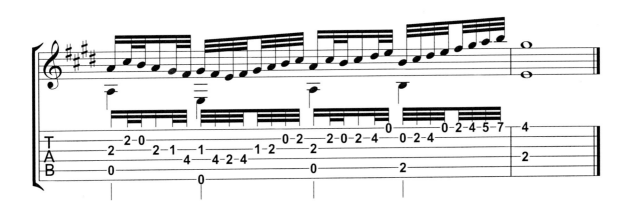

A 12 bar in A
with some double stops in 6ths

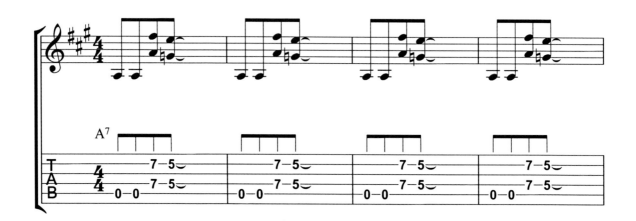

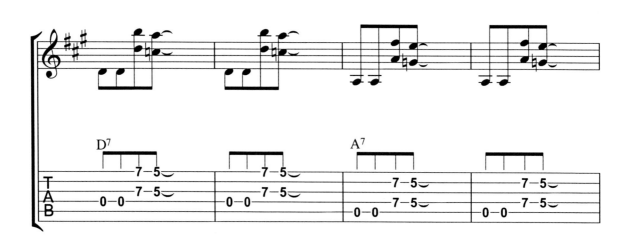

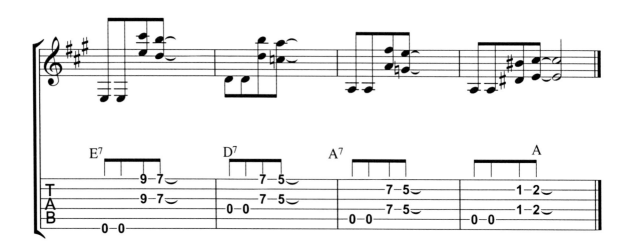

A 12 bar blues in A
with moveable chords and boogie bass fills

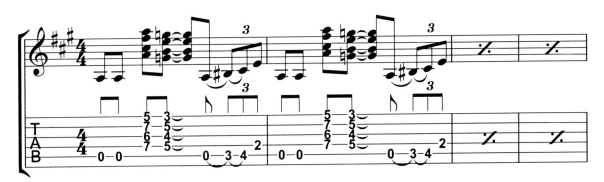

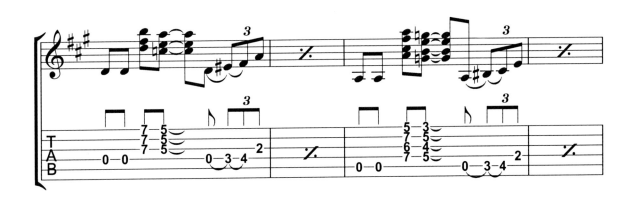

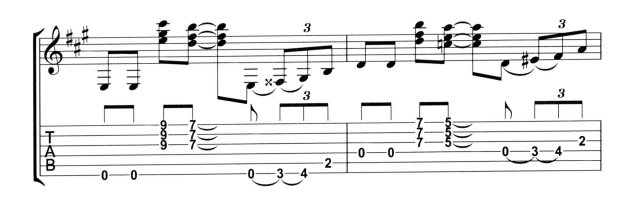

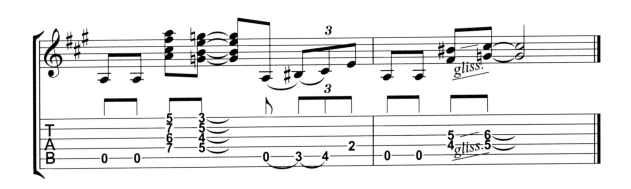

Valsette
see page 32 for duet version

See also pages 32, 64

harmonics

The Entertainer

Scott Joplin melody

as always with Scott Joplin
and ragtime: *not too fast*

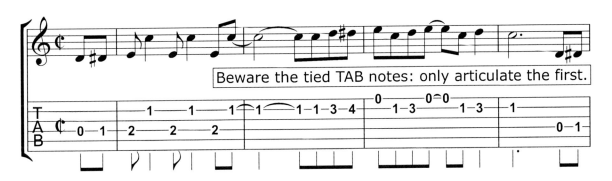

Beware the tied TAB notes: only articulate the first.

NB Sometimes TAB shows tied notes, sometimes just the one you play.

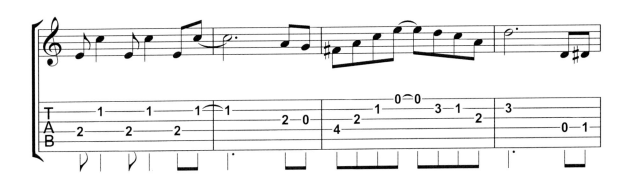

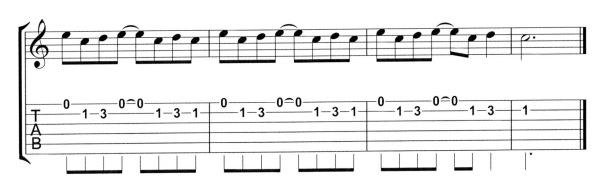

note reference chart:

music reading is a simple code

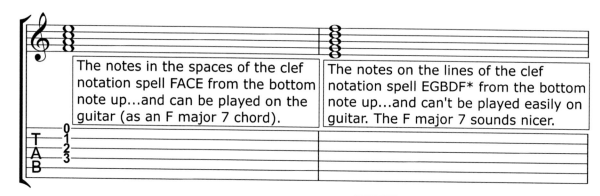

The notes in the spaces of the clef notation spell FACE from the bottom note up...and can be played on the guitar (as an F major 7 chord).

The notes on the lines of the clef notation spell EGBDF* from the bottom note up...and can't be played easily on guitar. The F major 7 sounds nicer.

*
**'Every Great Bear Deserves Fun'
- or make up your own to help
you remember.**

notes on string 1

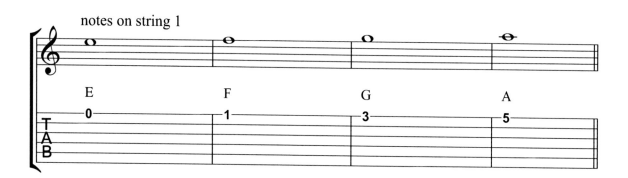

notes on string 2

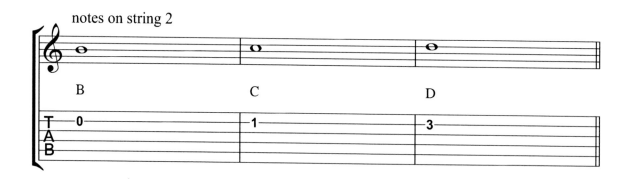

notes on string 3

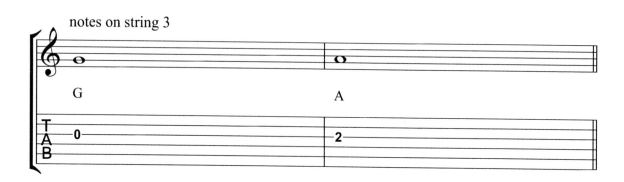

notes on string 4

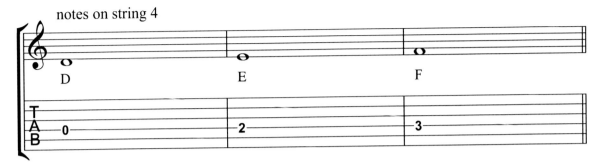

When the notes get too low for the stave, extra lines [leger, or ledger, lines] are used to help us identify them.

This is only necessary on the A [5th] and E [6th] strings.

notes on string 5

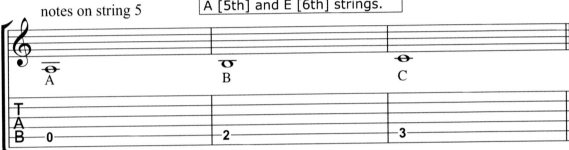

notes on string 6

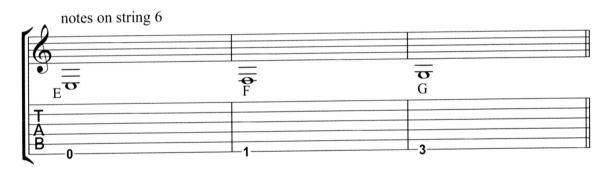

higher position notes

One of the joys - and a bugbear! - of the guitar is that you can often find the same notes in different places...

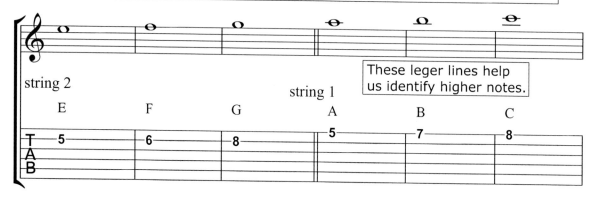

string 2

string 1

These leger lines help us identify higher notes.

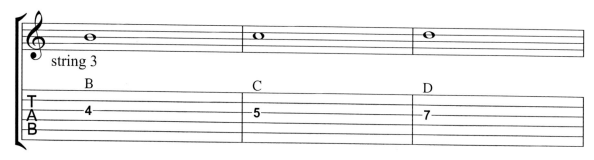

string 3

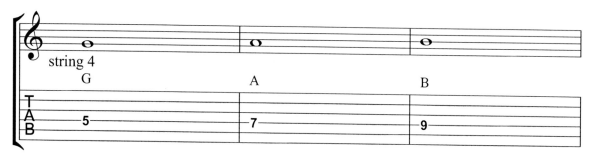

string 4

string 5

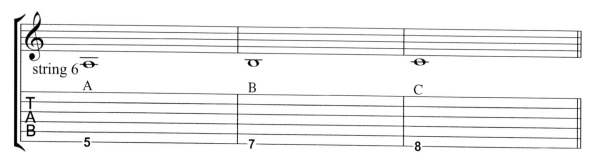

string 6

Amazing Grace with the 6th string dropped [tuned down] to D

Tune the bass string down until it 'agrees' with the D [4th] string but an octave lower.
It won't take a lot of turning of the tuning peg. The bottom three strings now sound like a drone.

64

A 'thumb & strum' sequence in E minor.
This works with *Valsette*.
The ∤ sign means do the same again.

See also
pages
32, 58

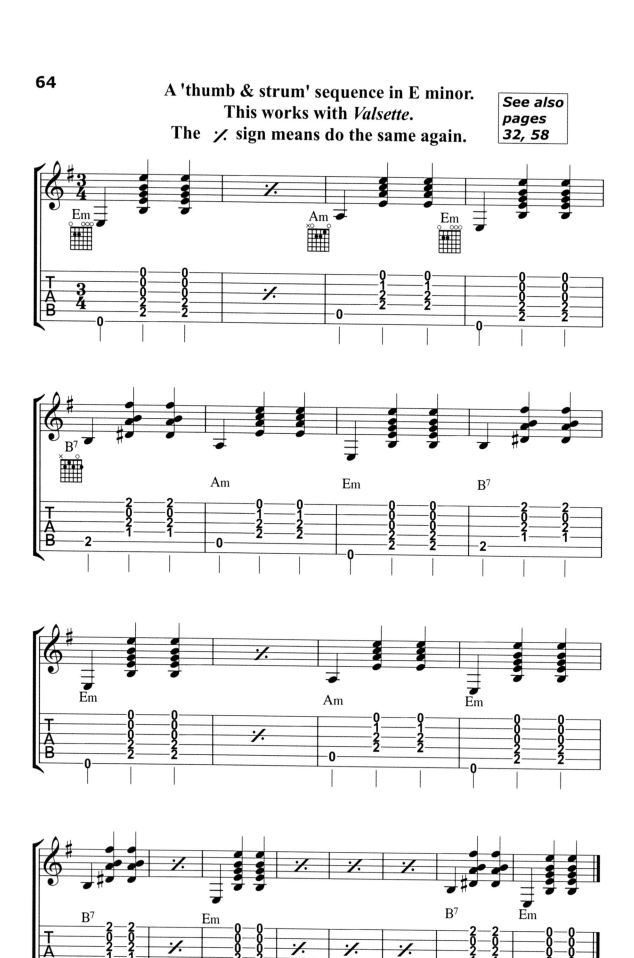

a low tune related to 'Blue Cannonball'

Got me on my knees

- a 'dead thumb' (repeated bass notes, often muted) blues
in 'drop' D tuning

On the move,
in the minor

in four parts: all, or any, parts work together as an ensemble piece

1.

Try it in swung rhythm

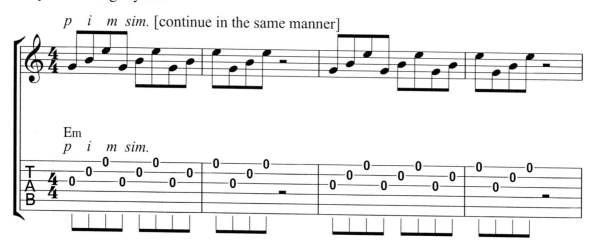

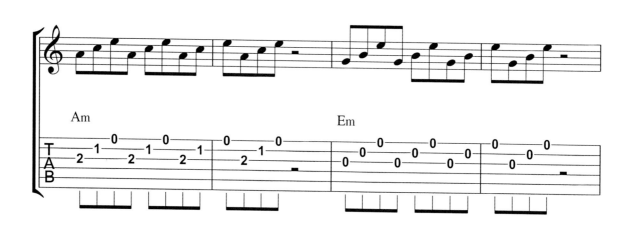

On the move,
in the minor
2.

On the move,
in the minor

3.

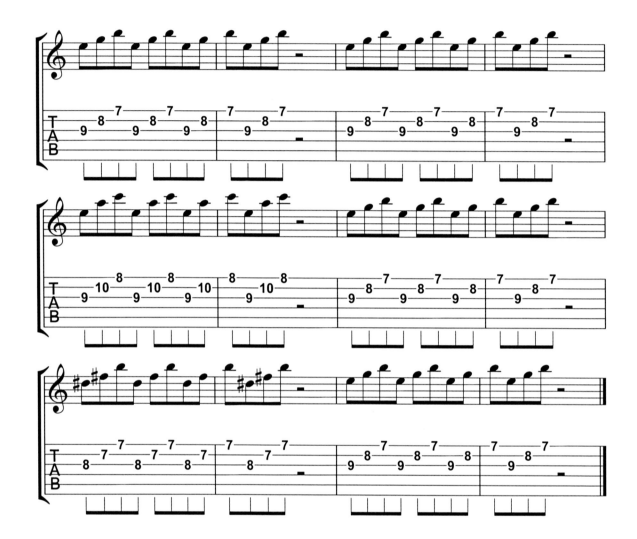

4. A latin style bass part for *On the Move In the Minor*

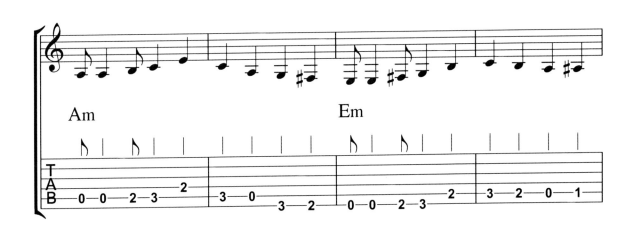

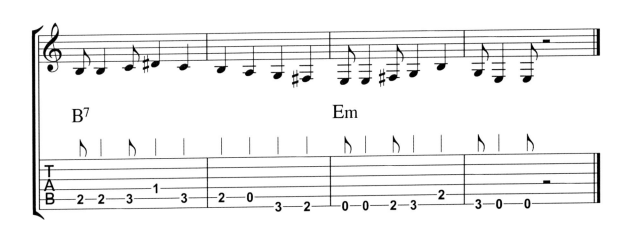

Chords are recipes of notes.
The ingredients of a common chord, or triad, are the 1st, 3rd and 5th notes of the scale.
Example: an A minor chord is made from the notes A, C and E.

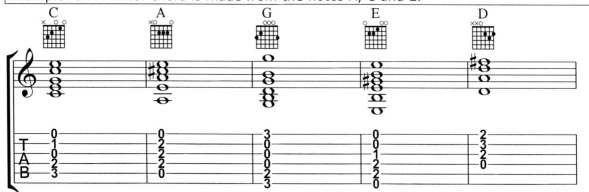

see pages 71 and 72 for
some other voicings of these

2. limited finger chords
- fancy names don't have to mean fancy fingerings!

See also page 9

this is a nice voicing

- play a bar of Em then a bar of this

- keep repeating and you are on the way to America's *Horse With No Name*

no third in this chord means it's neither major nor minor - or either...

3. moving the basics
once you have some finger memory, move those chords about

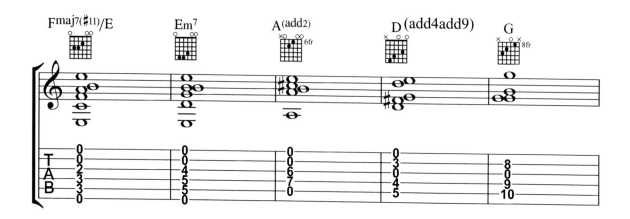

4. 5ths chords
'power chords'

In the hall of the mountain king

Grieg

It also works brilliantly in E minor - try palm-muting it!

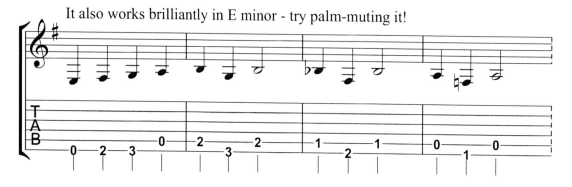

Caprice number 24
- theme

Paganini

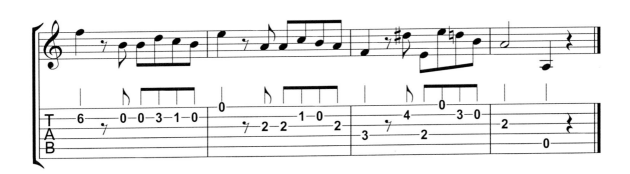

Winter
theme from The Four Seasons

Vivaldi

Winter
theme from The Four Seasons
another version - in D major

Sometimes it's interesting to explore what happens if we change key.

Vivaldi

Spring
theme from The Four Seasons

Vivaldi

with some higher position notes

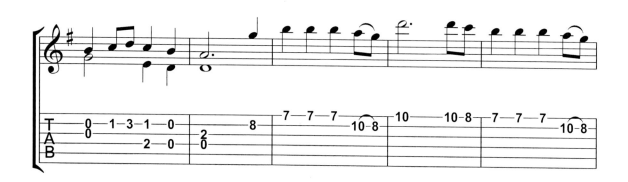

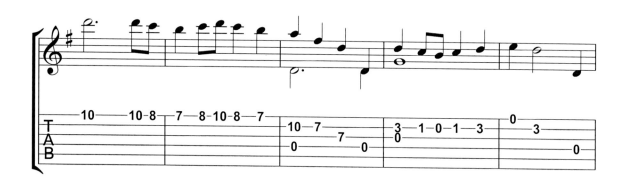

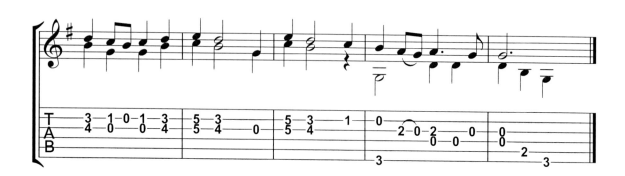

Space V2.0

an upgraded version of *BG workout*,
this is in Phrygian mode

Charlie Head

See also page 42

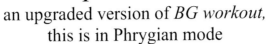

repeat **x 3**
sempre crescendo

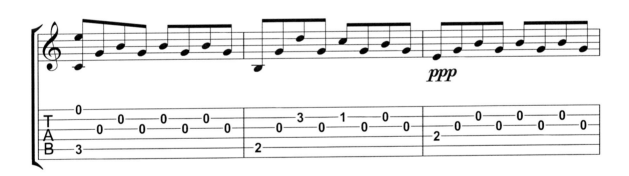

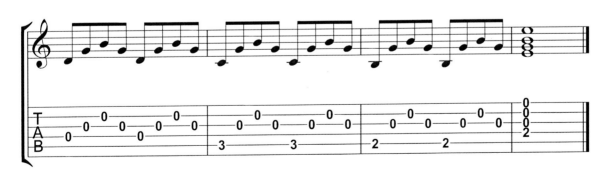

Lightning Source UK Ltd.
Milton Keynes UK
UKOW010608140513

210615UK00005B/174/P